MW01602258

Original title:

Shadows of the Mistwoven Glow

Copyright © 2025 Swan Charm

All rights reserved.

Author: Paula Raudsepp

ISBN HARDBACK: 978-9908-1-6397-0

ISBN PAPERBACK: 978-9908-1-6398-7

ISBN EBOOK: 978-9908-1-6399-4

The Veiled Path of Luminescent Dreams

In the hush of night's embrace,
Whispers echo soft and low.
Shadows dance with fleeting grace,
Where the silver rivers flow.

Glimmers trail through gentle mist,
Guiding hearts to paths unknown.
Every thought a wish to twist,
In the twilight's tranquil tone.

Figures glide on silver beams,
Threads of fate in quiet weave.
Through the veil of whispered dreams,
Where the soul learns to believe.

Light cascades on hidden trails,
Casting hopes in shades of gold.
Every sigh the silence sails,
Tales of truths that must be told.

On this path so freshly laid,
Each step echoes lost desires.
In the garden softly swayed,
Blooming bright like shooting fires.

Flickers of a Forgotten Glare

Beneath the arc of fading night,
Memories shimmer, pulse and sway.
Once they burned with fierce delight,
Now they flicker, fade away.

Past the echoes, lost in time,
Faintly glows a distant spark.
Each remembrance, pantomime,
Leaving traces in the dark.

Ancient shadows drawn in light,
Trace the forms of what once was.
Silent tales that hold tight,
To the spirit's fragile buzz.

Words unspoken, dreams displaced,
Lie within a hushed refrain.
Through the silence, dreams are chased,
Hoping to ignite the flame.

Yet in the gloom, a glimmer fights,
Stirring visions from the past.
Flickers dance on fragile lights,
Reminders that true love will last.

Enigmatic Gleams in the Haze

In the fog where secrets linger,
Whispers twist like vines around.
Glimmers tease the motion's finger,
Hiding truths that can't be found.

Shadows play in muted colors,
Formless shapes begin to breathe.
Lost in thoughts of silent suitors,
Glimmers brew beneath the sheath.

Every sparkle holds a story,
Crafted in the quiet seams.
Hints of glory, tales of worry,
Sown with hopes and distant dreams.

Through the haze, the heart can trace,
Paths that lead to hidden schemes.
In the dim, we find our place,
Covered still in shrouded beams.

Yet within this misty dance,
Hope ignites with fervent flame.
Through the fog, a fleeting chance,
Gleaming softly, yet the same.

Concealed in the Embrace of Twilight

Underneath the soft twilight,
Shadows blend with fading light.
Secrets whisper through the night,
As the stars begin their flight.

In this serene, enchanted space,
Magic weaves its gentle trace.
Time dissolves without a face,
Each heartbeat, a sweet embrace.

Memories wrapped in silver mist,
Draw us closer, hand in hand.
Every sigh, a fleeting kiss,
In this ever-shifting land.

Dreams entwined in twilight's glow,
Painting moments large and small.
In this hush, our spirits flow,
Unified through nightfall's call.

Wrapped in whispers soft and near,
Every heartbeat, love's refrain.
In this place devoid of fear,
Twilight cradles joy and pain.

Radiance of the Obscured

In shadows deep, a light does weave,
A whisper soft, that none believe.
Through veils of night, the stars break free,
A dance of dreams, a tapestry.

From hidden paths, the moonlight spills,
With silver threads, it gently fills.
The heart ignites with secrets shared,
In quiet realms, where souls have bared.

Through twilight's grace, the colors blend,
A brush of gold, as day must end.
The beauty lies in what we find,
In radiance spun by the blind.

Like fireflies that flicker, roam,
They guide the lost back toward home.
In shadows deep, hope still can gleam,
For even dark brings forth a dream.

The specter's glow guides wandering hearts,
A mystic glow that never departs.
Through obscured trails, we dare to tread,
With radiance soft, where fears have fled.

Murmurs of the Ethereal Shroud

Whispers float on a gentle breeze,
As twilight sings among the trees.
Veils of mist, so soft and thin,
Where secrets lie, and dreams begin.

In shimmering light, shadows play,
A realm where night dissolves to day.
Echoes dance in the silent gloom,
In every corner, a soft perfume.

In quiet sighs, the world unfolds,
With stories lost that time beholds.
Each murmur soft, a tale untold,
In ethereal shrouds, the brave grow bold.

The silver moon casts its gentle might,
Illuminating paths Through the night.
A sacred space for thoughts to drift,
In whispers shared, the spirit lifts.

Let hearts entwine with every breath,
As shadows mark the edge of death.
These murmurs hold the universe,
In ethereal shrouds, we pray and curse.

Tales Told by Misty Laughter

In misty trails, laughter rings clear,
Stories dance, drawing us near.
From the depths of fog, they arise,
With playful notes, under the skies.

Each chuckle holds a spark of light,
Chasing away the creeping night.
In dense embrace, spirits align,
A tapestry spun from threads divine.

Every giggle, a secret shared,
In evening's warmth, we're lightly spared.
Through nebulous veils, the tales unwind,
In misty laughter, joy we find.

With every whisper, a memory wakes,
In the heart's depths, the stillness breaks.
These tales of wonder, softly told,
In laughter wrapped, never grows old.

Let not the night silence the call,
For in our hearts, we shall not fall.
With misty laughter, dreams we weave,
In every tale, we dare believe.

Enigma of the Glimmering Dusk

At dusk, the sky begins to glow,
With hints of secrets that we know.
An enigma wrapped in evening's hue,
A canvas painted fresh and new.

The sun dips low, a fleeting glance,
As shadows deepen, the skies enhance.
Where colors blend, and thoughts entwine,
In glimmering dusk, our souls align.

In twilight's calm, we rest our minds,
Reflecting on what truth unwinds.
With gazes cast toward the west,
In enigma's grip, we find our rest.

A moment caught in still embrace,
The world feels lost in time and space.
In that brief fade between night and day,
There's magic found, in soft array.

Through the whispers of the autumn leaves,
An enigma hints at what believes.
In the glimmering dusk, we find our way,
As mysteries bloom at the end of day.

The Dance of Light and Fog

Shadows sway in gentle grace,
Whispers weave through fog's embrace.
A dance of dim and glowing sights,
The world transformed in faded lights.

Glistening trails of silver beams,
Mingle softly with the dreams.
Each step leads to unknown shores,
As fog envelops and restores.

Hidden paths beneath the haze,
Where time dissolves in misty gaze.
Light flickers in a playful jest,
Creating wonders on the crest.

As twilight melts to starry skies,
The fog retreats, the dance defies.
In this realm where shadows glide,
The heart of night is stirred with pride.

Hidden Rhapsody in the Palpable Night

In the depth of velvet skies,
Where silence reigns and true heart sighs.
A rhapsody unfolds untamed,
In moonlit tunes, the spirit's claimed.

Stars flicker softly, secrets share,
Every glance blooms with fragrant air.
The night enshrines such bewitching glow,
Painting dreams that ebb and flow.

Echoes linger, music's breath,
In shadows deep, we dance with death.
Every heartbeat, a solemn vow,
To cherish now, forget the how.

Night's embrace, a tender call,
Where hopes are sown and fears do fall.
In this hidden serenade,
Love and longing serenely braid.

Fabrics of Time Beneath Fading Glow

Threads of dusk entwine the day,
In whispered notes where moments play.
Fabrics woven with dreams anew,
Beneath the fading light's soft hue.

Every stitch holds tales untold,
Of laughter, whispers, glimmers bold.
As twilight melts in dusky bliss,
Time drapes gently, a fleeting kiss.

Here, memories flutter like moths,
In twilight's arms where silence cloths.
The future melds with distant past,
In every shadow, echoes cast.

As the glow begins to wane,
We find our beauty in the pain.
For threads of time, though worn and frayed,
In fading light, our hearts have played.

Secrets in the Veil of Dawn

Morning whispers through the trees,
Beneath the hush, a gentle breeze.
Veils of shadows start to part,
Revealing secrets to the heart.

The sun ascends, a golden hue,
Painting skies in vibrant blue.
Each ray a promise, soft and bright,
Awakening the sleeping night.

In the stillness, magic swirls,
A dance of light as nature twirls.
Dawn's canvas unfolds with grace,
Every stroke a warm embrace.

As dreams retreat, the day ignites,
In hues of amber, warm delights.
The veil is lifted, secrets shown,
In dawn's embrace, we are not alone.

Chasing Echoes in the Misty Embrace

In shadows soft, whispers call,
The night unfolds, a velvet thrall.
Footsteps dance on silent ground,
Chasing echoes that astound.

Moonlight weaves through trees so tall,
Each heartbeat echoes, a distant thrall.
The mist cloaks dreams in subtle grace,
As stars reflect on time's face.

Waves of fog wrap tightly 'round,
Lost in the peace, I'm spellbound.
With each breath, the night I trace,
Carried forward in time's embrace.

A whispered sigh, a fleeting glance,
In this moment, shadows dance.
Chasing echoes through the night,
Lost in dreams, out of sight.

Guided by the stars above,
I find solace, I find love.
In the mist, where secrets lie,
Chasing echoes, I learn to fly.

Between the Layers of Twilight Glow

Between the layers of twilight hue,
A world awakes, calm and new.
Soft whispers blend with colors bold,
In this hour, stories unfold.

The sky spills gold, a gentle rush,
While shadows play in evening's hush.
Leaves rustle under breezes light,
Bathed in warmth, the stars ignite.

In the stillness, dreams take flight,
Merging day with the coming night.
Each heartbeat syncs with nature's flow,
Between the layers, magic grows.

Footsteps linger on paths unknown,
Embracing moments softly sown.
In the dance of dusk's embrace,
We find our place, we find our grace.

From dusk till dawn, in twilight's glow,
The heart remembers, the spirit knows.
In the twilight, we discover,
Between the layers, we're all lovers.

The Gaze of Faded Brilliance

In shadows deep, the memories lie,
Flickers of gold in the evening sky.
Once they danced, now they softly fade,
The gaze of brilliance, a time once made.

Whispers of light from the past still call,
Echoes of laughter that linger, enthrall.
A tapestry woven with threads of grace,
In the heart's quiet vault, they find their place.

Under the moon's gentle, silver gaze,
Faded brilliance wraps the world in a haze.
The stars reminisce of stories told,
While time softly weaves their secrets of old.

With every glance, a journey begins,
To places where silence and solace spins.
Carried away on the winds of night,
In the heart of the dark, there's a flicker of light.

So let us cherish the moments defined,
By faded brilliance our hearts entwined.
In every sigh, a piece of our past,
In the gaze of the night, memories last.

Woven Whispers Beyond the Dim

In the twilight's embrace, whispers arise,
Soft threads of twilight weave into the skies.
Each vow carried by the breath of the night,
Woven in silence, a tapestry bright.

Beyond the shadows where dreams dare to roam,
The echoes of laughter remind us of home.
Gentle are voices that float through the air,
Speaking of wonders that linger with care.

Stars bloom like blossoms in the muted dark,
Whispers entwined with the night's sacred spark.
While secrets exchange on the breeze like a sigh,
Woven together, our hopes learn to fly.

In gatherings hushed, where the heartbeats sync,
We linger in moments, just enough to think.
Each glance a promise, a bond we hold dear,
In woven whispers, the world feels clear.

So let us listen to the stories they tell,
Beyond the dim light, where shadows dwell.
For in every murmur, a universe waits,
Woven in whispers, our fate resonates.

A Symphony of Muted Light

When day turns to dusk, a symphony starts,
In the gentle embrace of shared beating hearts.
Muted hues blend, a soft serenade,
Illuminated dreams where fears start to fade.

Strings of the twilight, they pluck at our souls,
An orchestra sings, as dusk gently rolls.
The warmth of the fading sun melts away,
Creating a canvas where shadows can play.

Notes drift like feathers, so tender and clear,
In a soft harmony, we lean in to hear.
Each moment a pulse, each sigh a refrain,
A symphony woven through joy and through pain.

The stars join the chorus, the cosmos aligns,
As the night wraps its arms in delicate signs.
Together we dance in this hush of the night,
Floating on melodies, lost in the light.

In every heartbeat, a story unfolds,
A symphony gathered, like whispers of old.
We cherish the notes, let the music ignite,
In the symphony formed of this muted light.

Translucent Serenades at Dusk

Where the sky meets the horizon, colors collide,
Translucent serenades begin their glide.
Soft echoes of twilight, a whisper so sweet,
Brush strokes of nature, a rhythm discrete.

In the gentle unfolding of night's embrace,
Dance of the fireflies, a lithe, airy grace.
Each twinkle a note in a melodic stream,
Painting the dusk with a shadowy dream.

Leaves rustle softly, an undulating song,
In harmony woven where we all belong.
The breeze carries tales of the day's warm sigh,
Translucent serenades breathe life in the sky.

As the stars pierce the fabric with glimmers of light,
Our spirits take flight in the softening night.
Each heartbeat a moment, each moment a kiss,
Translucent serenades weave a tale of bliss.

In the hush that follows, let our hearts align,
To the music of dusk, a love so divine.
Together we linger, the world pauses near,
In translucent serenades, we find our clear.

A Serenade for the Misty Morn

Softly rises the golden hue,
As shadows stretch and dance anew.
Whispers of dawn in the gentle air,
Nature awakens, free from care.

Crickets fade with the night's retreat,
Birds begin their morning greet.
A rustling breeze in the swaying trees,
Teases the mist like a soft caress.

Sunbeams pierce the silken veil,
A tale of beauty that won't fail.
Petals bloom in radiant light,
Emerging from the depths of night.

The day unfolds a canvas bright,
Guiding warmth in the soft sunlight.
Each breath a melody, pure and sweet,
Mornings dance to a rhythmic beat.

In quiet moments, time stands still,
Embraced by nature's tender thrill.
A serenade for the misty morn,
Where every soul is reborn.

Veils of Luminous Whisper

In twilight's embrace, the night takes flight,
Veils of whispers cloaked in light.
Stars awaken, twinkling bright,
A silent hymn to the velvet night.

Moonbeams weave a silver thread,
Through dreams where the lost souls tread.
Each flicker tells a tale profound,
In shadows deep, new worlds are found.

Gentle sighs of the nightingale,
Echo in hearts, a haunting tale.
With every note, a wish takes form,
In veils of luminous, soft and warm.

Whispers dance on the cool night air,
Memories linger, woven with care.
In the hush, a secret shared,
In this silence, souls are bared.

Veils of light in the night unfold,
Stories of love that never grow old.
In the land where shadows sleep,
Dreams awaken, promises keep.

Echoes in the Haze

In a world wrapped in silver gray,
Echoes of laughter drift away.
Whispers of time in soft embrace,
Floating gently, a fleeting trace.

Through the mist, a soft refrain,
Haunting notes of joy and pain.
Memories linger like morning dew,
In the haze, old dreams renew.

Faces blur in the softest light,
Fleeting visions in day and night.
Echoing love in breath and sigh,
In the stillness, spirits fly.

Gentle waves of the unseen past,
Flow like rivers that ever last.
In the haze, we find our way,
With echoes guiding our hearts to stay.

So let the mist kiss every thought,
In the haze, life's lessons taught.
For in each whisper, hope entwines,
Echoes of love in endless lines.

Dances of Forgotten Light

In corners where shadows tread,
Dances of light, where dreams are led.
Flickers of joy in the cloudy dusk,
Whispers of hope in the gentle husk.

Lonely stars in the velvet night,
Shimmer with tales of ancient flight.
Each sparkle sings of forgotten days,
As memory twirls in a delicate haze.

Beneath the moon's soft silver gaze,
Hearts remember in the warm embrace.
Dances begin with the night's sweet call,
Awakening spirits after all.

Footprints linger on sands of time,
In every beat, a silent rhyme.
With every twirl, we find our peace,
Dances of light that never cease.

Hold close the moments, let them ignite,
In the fabric of dreams, they shine bright.
For in the night's tender delight,
We become part of the dances of light.

Dancers in the Twilight Embrace

In the calm of fading light,
Whispers twirl like shadows' flight,
Silhouettes in soft hue sway,
Lost in dusk till end of day.

An echo of a fleeting song,
Hearts entwined where few belong,
Every step, a tender grace,
In this twilight's warm embrace.

Glimmers sparkle like sweet dreams,
Every breath, a gentle theme,
As the stars begin to gleam,
Dancers weave a twilight seam.

With the night unfold their plans,
Holding close in secret hands,
Each move a promise, soft and true,
In twilight's glow, they both renew.

Underneath the velvet sky,
Where the muted shadows lie,
They lose sight of time and space,
Dancing slow in twilight's grace.

Allure of the Luminous Veil

Beneath the moon's soft, silver light,
A veil of dreams begins to write,
Stories spun from starlit threads,
Whispered secrets, softly spread.

In the shroud of midnight's glow,
Laughter echoes, soft and low,
With each twirl, a magic spell,
Caught within the luminous swell.

The night unveils its gentle charm,
Wrapped in shadows, safe from harm,
Every flicker brings a sigh,
As spirits dance, the world awry.

Lights entwine like lovers' grace,
In this dreamy, sacred space,
Every heartbeat blends with light,
Illuminated, lost in night.

In the silence, hear the call,
A beckoning to one and all,
In the glow, our souls unveil,
Enticed by the luminous veil.

Mystique of the Dusky Glow

In the amber light of night,
Softly echoes of delight,
Shadows dance in rhythmic play,
Cloaked in mystique's warm array.

Every moment, time stands still,
As hearts pulse with quiet thrill,
Embers flicker, stories rise,
In the dusky glow, surprise.

Underneath the starlit sky,
Whispered wishes linger by,
Crafting stories in the dark,
Each a spark, each a mark.

Swaying to the night's soft tune,
Beneath the watchful silver moon,
Lives entwined in dusk's gentle flow,
Caught in the mystique, we grow.

As the night begins to wane,
Memories, like echoes, reign,
Held within the dusky glow,
Where hearts linger, soft and slow.

Wandering through the Misted Dreams

In the haze of morning light,
Footsteps wander, soft, polite,
Misted dreams begin to rise,
Veiling secrets, hearts surprise.

Through the fog where shadows wade,
Emotions dance, and thoughts cascade,
Eager whispers, soft and low,
Guide the way where dreamers go.

Every pathway, filled with grace,
Leads us to a hidden place,
Where the world feels far away,
In this mist, our spirits play.

Time dissolves in currents deep,
Carried forth on winds that sweep,
Floating long like drifting streams,
Wandering through the misted dreams.

And as the dawn begins to break,
The taming light, our hearts awake,
Yet in dreams, we still shall roam,
Wandering, forever home.

Dance of the Half-Seen Specter

In shadows soft where whispers play,
A flicker moves, then slips away.
The moonlight casts its silver grin,
In silence deep, the dance begins.

Phantom feet on cobblestone,
Echoes of a world unknown.
Twists and turns without a sound,
In twilight's grip, the lost are found.

A gentle sway in misty strands,
Fingers brush like woven bands.
In every step, a timeless trace,
Of bygone tales in this still space.

The specter's grace, a fleeting glance,
Entwined in evening's hazy dance.
With each movement, secrets spill,
A haunting charm that lingers still.

Beneath the stars, a secret pact,
Where hearts of stone embrace the fact.
In memory's embrace, we cling,
To shadows waltzing, whispering.

Where the Light Meets the Veil

Glimmers rise at the edge of night,
Where dreams converge with fading light.
A soft caress of amber glow,
In the quiet, secrets grow.

Mist lingers, a gentle sigh,
Hiding truths as moments fly.
The horizon blushes, soft and pale,
Where the light meets the thin veil.

Footsteps echo on unseen ground,
In this hush, the lost are found.
Through whispers woven with the past,
Each heartbeat holds the shadows fast.

A fleeting beam of soft reprieve,
Guides the souls who dare to believe.
In twilight's reach, the shadows twine,
As light and veils in union shine.

Tomorrow waits just out of sight,
In the balance of day and night.
Forever seeking, always near,
The dance of light, both bright and sheer.

A Glimmer in the Weave of Dusk

The dusk unfolds in woven hues,
A tapestry of fading blues.
Among the threads, a flicker glows,
A glimmer where the mystery flows.

Shadows stretch, they twist and bend,
In twilight's arms, we find our friend.
A soft embrace, a lingering sigh,
In this moment, we learn to fly.

The whispers speak of things unseen,
Of lost desires and what has been.
With each heartbeat, the fabric shifts,
As time unwinds and slowly lifts.

A spark ignites in the twilight's grip,
With every breath, the night's love dips.
Colors merge in a gentle waltz,
Where all the world's forgotten faults.

In dusk, we weave our dreams anew,
With silver threads and hints of blue.
Forever caught in this embrace,
A glimmer shines in time's vast space.

Melodies Adrift in Luminous Haze

Soft notes drift on a velvet breeze,
In luminous haze, the heart finds ease.
The moonlight hums a haunting tune,
Inviting dreams beneath the moon.

Laughter echoes through the night,
Weaving joy in shimmering light.
Each star, a note in cosmic play,
As melodies guide the lost away.

In every whisper, stories dwell,
The magic spun, a woven spell.
Through gentle chords, we start to glide,
In this hush, our fears abide.

Fingers dance on strings so fine,
Creating waves where hearts entwine.
Lost in sound, we drift and sway,
In luminous haze, we find our way.

A serenade for sleepless souls,
In this moment, the world consoles.
With every breath, our spirits rise,
Melodies adrift beneath the skies.

Ghosts of Brilliance in the Mist

In the dawn's soft glow, whispers arise,
Shadows of dreams, where memory lies.
Echoes of laughter, fading away,
In the quiet dawn, they softly sway.

Flickers of light, through the shroud they weave,
Ghosts of brilliance, in the morn they cleave.
Draped in the mist, they dance and play,
A spectral embrace that won't decay.

Lingering sighs of a bygone age,
Pages of life, turn with the sage.
Threads of the past, softly entwined,
In the heart of the mist, beauty defined.

Among every shadow, a tale remains,
Whispered secrets, like gentle rains.
Each droplet holds, a moment's grace,
In the misty hues, we find our place.

For even in silence, brilliance can gleam,
Ghosts walk beside us, woven in dreams.
Their laughter and light guide us along,
In the mist's embrace, we are all strong.

Wandering Through the Cloaked Luminescence

In twilight's embrace, the shadows dance,
A mystery calls, so sweet the chance.
Pathways shimmer in silvery light,
Cloaked in the hues of the coming night.

Footfalls echo on the ancient ground,
The pulse of the earth, a haunting sound.
Wandering souls in the fading warm glow,
Through cloaked luminescence, we aim to know.

Flickering fireflies weave stories untold,
Secrets of the night, in their light bold.
Calmness surrounds, as time slips away,
In this shimmering world, we dare to stay.

Beneath the stars, a quiet refrain,
A song of the lost, a dance in the rain.
In the cloak of the night, we find our dreams,
Far from the light, where magic redeems.

We wander on paths, both ancient and new,
In cloaked luminescence, hearts beat true.
Together we seek, through whispers and sighs,
Under the veil, where the mystery lies.

The Path of Unseen Radiance

Step softly upon the hidden way,
Where light and shadows dance and play.
Unseen radiance guides each footfall,
In the quiet moments, we hear the call.

Faint glimmers linger in the twilight haze,
Drawing us near with their delicate gaze.
The path unfolds in whispers of light,
Each step, a promise in the deepening night.

Beneath the arching branches, hearts opens wide,
In the rustling leaves, secrets abide.
The unseen radiance, a gentle guide,
Illuminates the way where dreams reside.

With every breath, we embrace the night,
The path of radiance, welcoming light.
In the dance of shadows, we find our way,
Through the unseen, we choose to stay.

And as the stars begin to shine bright,
We wander on, hearts full of light.
For the path we walk, though oft unseen,
Is painted with magic, vibrant and clean.

Fading Glories in the Misty Veil

In the twilight's grasp, glories decay,
Whispers of splendor, drifting away.
Misty veils hide the tales once bold,
Fading memories, like threads of gold.

Glistening echoes, where laughter thrived,
In the misty embrace, old dreams survived.
Haunting the silence, they yearn for the day,
Fading glories, forever at play.

Underneath the shrouded twilight sky,
Each fading moment, a soft lullaby.
With every breath, we remember the light,
In the misty veil, they flicker from sight.

Through the hazy dawn, shadows will drift,
Carrying whispers, a bittersweet gift.
Fading spectacles in memory's haze,
Forever entwined in the evening's rays.

And as the light dims, we softly reflect,
On fading glories we cannot forget.
In the mist's quiet dance, we'll always find,
The beauty of memories, sweetly entwined.

Lurkers of the Misty Affection

In shadows deep, they quietly dwell,
Murmurs of love in a hidden shell.
Soft whispers weave through the foggy night,
Lurkers of affection, hidden from sight.

Beneath the haze, their secrets entwine,
Fleeting glances, a touch of divine.
The heartbeats echo, a delicate thread,
In the mist, where soft dreams are fed.

Glimmers of hope in a blurred embrace,
In silence they dance, a gentle grace.
Misty veils cloak the warmth of their sighs,
In the depths of shadows, passion lies.

Caught in the moment, time stands still,
Lurkers of longing, bound by will.
A radiant pulse in the twilight's bloom,
Their hearts awaken in quiet gloom.

Unseen they wander, a spectral parade,
In the misty veil, love's masquerade.
The night unfolds, secrets held dear,
In liquidity's shimmer, they linger near.

Threads of Light in the Hazy Darkness

In a realm of shadows, glimmers arise,
Threads of light that paint the skies.
Through hazy darkness, they bravely weave,
Illuminating paths for those who believe.

Fleeting moments catch the eye,
Dancing softly, they twirl and fly.
Each ray a whisper, a story untold,
Threads of connection that never grow cold.

In the ether, where dreams take flight,
They guide lost souls through the endless night.
A tapestry woven with colors so bright,
Threads of hope in the inky plight.

Beneath the veils of obscured sight,
A shimmer of love in the heart's delight.
In tangled trails, we find our way,
Threads of light, forever to stay.

Awakening hearts in slumber's embrace,
Kissed by the grace of a luminous trace.
In the night's embrace, we find our spark,
Threads of light illuminating the dark.

Veils of Radiant Secrets

In layers soft, the secrets hide,
Veils of light on the dark side.
Whispers linger in the cool breeze,
Radiant truths, igniting at ease.

Each shimmering strand tells a tale,
Songs of heart, a gentle hail.
In twilight's embrace, they softly unfold,
Veils of radiant secrets, a mystery bold.

Silken shadows caress the dawn,
In the silence, a fresh song drawn.
Glimmers of truth in the brightening skies,
Secrets emerge as the daylight flies.

In frosted webs, they bloom like flowers,
Revealing the magic of hidden powers.
Resonant echoes of loves once lost,
Veils unmask emotions, no matter the cost.

With every flutter, the spirits soar,
Unveiling the treasures we can't ignore.
In the heart's realm, where dreams entwine,
Veils of radiant secrets, forever divine.

Elusive Glows in the Unseen

In the depth of night, faint glimmers glow,
Elusive whispers, soft and slow.
Hidden from view, they spark a fire,
In the unseen realms of our heart's desire.

Through the silence, wonders blink,
Melodies echo, making us think.
Each star a secret, each smile serene,
Elusive glows in a world between.

With every hint of twilight's grace,
We wander through dreams, a timeless space.
Where shadows dance and feelings ignite,
Elusive glows bring warmth to the night.

Fragile as webs, yet strong like steel,
In the dark, they twinkle and feel.
Guiding the way for lost souls to glean,
Elusive glows in the tapestry unseen.

In the fabric of night, we find our part,
Illuminated threads that join every heart.
For in the unseen, our spirits convene,
Elusive glows, where love reigns supreme.

The Specter of a Shimmering Mist

In twilight's grasp, a phantom glows,
A dance of shadows, where no one goes.
Whispers travel on the cool, crisp air,
Hints of secrets linger everywhere.

Veils of silver wrap the world in dreams,
Echoes of laughter, or so it seems.
Each breath of wind tells tales untold,
Of moments cherished, memories bold.

Glimmers of light through the fabric weave,
Chasing the darkness that wishes to cleave.
A shimmering presence, both near and far,
Shaping our night like a guiding star.

In the stillness, a hush takes flight,
Softly cradling the veil of night.
The specter fades with the rise of dawn,
Leaving behind a world reborn.

As morning breaks with a gentle sigh,
The shimmering mist begins to dry.
Yet in our hearts, the memory stays,
Of twilight's magic in wondrous ways.

Mysteries Wreathed in Fog

A shroud of gray envelopes the ground,
Where nature's secrets are tightly bound.
Footsteps falter on the dampened earth,
Cradling whispers of ancient birth.

In the charm of dusk, the fog descends,
Painting the world where mystery blends.
Figures emerge, then are lost from sight,
Navigating shadows with pure delight.

The trees stand tall, like guardians wise,
Holding the stories of the ages' rise.
Through tendrils of mist, the moonlight streams,
Draping the land in a tapestry of dreams.

Voices linger, in the stillness heard,
Murmurs of legends, soft and blurred.
Each breath of fog conceals and reveals,
A world enchanted, where time gently heals.

In the heart of night, the mysteries play,
Wreathed in sentiment, lost in sway.
As dawn approaches, the secrets break,
Yet the echo of magic will never forsake.

Reflections of the Hidden Glow

Beneath the surface, a quiet light,
Glimmers softly, hidden from sight.
In pools of silence, dreams intertwine,
Whispers of hope in shadows divine.

Mirrored waters catch the waning stars,
Shimmering echoes of distant Mars.
Gaze deeper still, let your spirit flow,
Through reflections of the hidden glow.

Ripples of longing dance on the tide,
Caressing the edges where secrets bide.
In each minute stir, a story unfolds,
Tales of the heart, both timid and bold.

The night reveals what the day conceals,
Emotions bare, the soul reveals.
Softly woven in a silver thread,
Every moment captures what's unsaid.

As dawn breaks through the veil of night,
Reflections shimmer with nascent light.
Embrace the day, let the shadows go,
And cherish the tales that the night will show.

Veiling the Echoes of Night

In the shroud where silence clings,
Veiling echoes of forgotten things.
The stars hum softly to the waiting skies,
While shadows march with secret sighs.

Moonlight drips like liquid gold,
Mapping the stories that fate has told.
Each pulse of night wraps around my soul,
As darkness whispers, and shadows roll.

Footsteps echo on the cobbled street,
The rhythm of hearts, a steady beat.
In the corners of dreams, enchantments lie,
Tracing the paths where stories fly.

With every breath, the night unfolds,
A tapestry woven with threads of gold.
Veiling secrets, in shadows cast,
Binding the future with whispers of past.

As dawn calls forth with a gentle blaze,
The echoes retreat in the morning haze.
Yet the essence of night lingers still,
In the heart's quiet, whispering thrill.

Luminescent Whispers in the Fog

Whispers drift through the cool night air,
Mist weaves tales in a silvery snare.
Stars blink softly, ancient and wise,
Secrets hide where the darkness lies.

Shadows dance in the shrouded light,
Echoes of dreams take flight in the night.
Each breath a story of lost and found,
In fog's embrace, our hearts are bound.

Moonlight filters through the parched trees,
Lending its glow to the gentle breeze.
Every corner holds a waiting sigh,
In the foggy lace, we learn to fly.

Carried away on the currents of thought,
Whispers of hope in the battles fought.
Lanterns glow softly, guiding the way,
In this dance of light, we choose to stay.

A tender hush wraps the world so tight,
Wrapped in whispers, lost to the night.
Together we wander, forever we'll roam,
Finding our solace in fog's gentle home.

Veiled Glint of Enchanted Twilight

Twilight weaves a canopy bright,
Veils of magic take their flight.
Colors blend in a soft embrace,
Shadows linger, a fleeting trace.

A whisper floats on the evening breeze,
Enticing dreams beneath the trees.
Stars peek out with a glimmering glow,
Painting the sky in a lover's show.

Glimmers of hope in the gathering shade,
Illuminating paths the heart has made.
Each heartbeat echoes promises sweet,
Under twilight's watch, we find our beat.

Through the thicket, a sigh drifts free,
Songs of the night call out to thee.
Moments captured in whispers' flight,
Veiled in the charm of enchanted night.

Time stands still in this sacred place,
Veiled glint of twilight, a soft embrace.
Together we dream in the twilight hue,
Forever lost in the magic of you.

A Tapestry Woven by Moonlight

Moonlight spills like silk on the floor,
Threads of silver, ancient lore.
Every glimmer tells a tale,
A tapestry rich, where dreams set sail.

Stars are the weavers of night's design,
Stitching the sky with a delicate line.
In this art of darkness, shadows play,
Creating a world where night meets day.

Every sigh holds a moment's grace,
Woven in whispers, finding our place.
The fabric of time folds soft and slow,
Bathed in moon's light, our spirits glow.

Patterns emerge in the quiet so deep,
Visions unravel, secrets to keep.
In the embrace of this luminous night,
We find ourselves in the stillness of light.

With every heartbeat, the story unfolds,
A tapestry woven, colors bold.
Together we dream under celestial beams,
In moonlight's glow, we discover our dreams.

Grace of the Shimmering Shadows

In the hush of night, shadows breathe,
A graceful dance, they weave and seethe.
Edges smooth in the twilight's grace,
Whispers of night in a soft embrace.

Glistening softly, like dew on grass,
Moments linger, as seconds pass.
The world transforms under shimmering light,
Graceful silhouettes take joyous flight.

Beneath the stars, shadows intertwine,
Echoing stories through passion's line.
In every shape, a journey untold,
Grace of the night, pure and bold.

As moonbeam fingers brush their skin,
A tale unfolds where we both begin.
Together we wander, lost in the glow,
In the shimmering shadows, we learn and grow.

The night embraces with tender care,
Every heartbeat ignites in the air.
Grace of the shadows, night's gentle song,
In this sacred dance, we both belong.

Veil of Whispering Light

In the dawn's gentle embrace,
Shadows dance, time slows its race.
Colors bloom with soft delight,
A world reborn in whispering light.

Petals flutter, secrets shared,
On the breeze, dreams are bared.
Golden rays grace the earth,
A symphony of silent mirth.

Voices rise from the green below,
Nature's hymn, a sweet echo.
Each leaf sings of love's tether,
In this veil, we are forever.

The brook babbles ancient tales,
While the heart knows never fails.
Hope unfurls in every sight,
Wrapped in the veil of whispering light.

Stars will watch as night descends,
Guiding paths where the journey bends.
Even when darkness takes flight,
We find peace in that soft light.

Echoes in the Haze

In the stillness, whispers sound,
Secrets linger, lost but found.
Through the mist, shadows roam,
Every echo finds its home.

Footsteps trace forgotten trails,
Memories dance, the heart prevails.
Fleeting moments in the night,
Wrapped in the warmth of dimmed light.

Voices mingle in the air,
Tales of love, joy, and despair.
Each word drifts like a sigh,
Carried softly, by and by.

In the haze, we come alive,
Each breath shared helps us thrive.
Time stands still; we rejoice,
In the echo of a single voice.

Fading light through trees of old,
Whispers turn to stories bold.
Together, we dance with grace,
In the haze, we find our place.

Dreams Entwined in Twilight

As day gives way to night's embrace,
Shadows merge in a tender space.
Whispers of dreams painting the sky,
Where wishes linger, floating high.

Stars awaken with secret gleam,
Cradling our thoughts in a gentle dream.
Each heartbeat sings to the stars above,
Entwining souls, binding love.

The moon's soft glow, a silken thread,
Woven tight where stories are fed.
In twilight's arms, we share our fears,
While laughter mingles with falling tears.

Endless moments stretch and bend,
In this space where worlds transcend.
Together, we find our flight,
Our dreams entwined in twilight light.

With gentle breath, we drift away,
In the twilight, we find our stay.
Hand in hand, we share the night,
Chasing dreams till morning's light.

Luminance beneath the Gloom

In shadows deep where silence breeds,
Hope flickers softly, planting seeds.
Amidst the dark, a light shines through,
A gentle glow, both calm and true.

The weight of night may draw us low,
But deep within, a fire aglow.
Thinking of warmth in cold, dark rooms,
We find our strength, dispelling glooms.

Stars will blink in skies awash,
Inspiration blooms from every quash.
Each flicker whispers, 'You are brave,'
In1 the dark, still, we can pave.

Memory fires against the frost,
Though moments fade, we count the cost.
Yet from the ashes, we'll revive,
Finding luminance, we survive.

Through the trials, light will seep,
In every heart, the shadows keep.
Beneath the gloom, we rise and sway,
Towards the dawn of a brighter day.

Wandering Through the Gossamer Glow

Through the mist, I drift and sway,
In the twilight, shadows play.
Whispers linger in the breeze,
Carried softly by the trees.

Moonlit paths, a silver sheen,
Echoes dance where none have been.
Stars awaken, skies ignite,
Guiding me through endless night.

Footsteps light on velvet ground,
In this world, lost and found.
Every turn, a story told,
In the glow of dreams of old.

Waves of color sweep the dark,
Illuminating each small spark.
With every breath, I feel alive,
As the whispers start to thrive.

Gossamer threads of fate entwine,
Leading me with a subtle sign.
In the hush, serenity sings,
Wandering through what evening brings.

Whispering Hues Beneath the Twilight

Colors blend in gentle streams,
Painting softly through my dreams.
Beneath the sky, a canvas bare,
Whispers linger in the air.

Twilight paints the world anew,
With shades of gold and muted blue.
Dancing lights, a symphony,
Calling forth sweet memory.

Underneath the vibrant glow,
Nature's heartbeat, soft and slow.
Every hue a secret told,
In the twilight, dreams unfold.

Silhouetted figures blend,
As day and night begin to mend.
Breath of dusk, so sweetly spun,
Lullabies of day now done.

In the hush, the stars emerge,
Rising soft with twilight's urge.
Whispering hues, a tender night,
Holding close the fading light.

The Lure of Obscured Brilliance

Beneath the depth of shadowed skies,
Lies a spark that never dies.
Hidden gems await the glance,
In darkness, they begin to dance.

Gentle echoes of the past,
Call me forth, their voice steadfast.
In the mystery of the night,
Brilliance lies out of sight.

The moon a guide through velvet waves,
Leading to the truth it saves.
Every heartbeat, quiet plea,
Lure of brilliance sets me free.

In shadows deep, the secrets twine,
With every step, stars redefine.
A longing glow, a fate entwined,
In obscured realms, hope I find.

The darkness whispers, soft and low,
Learn from shadows, let them show.
With open heart, the night will teach,
Obscured brilliance, always within reach.

Ghostly Threads of Shimmering Light

In the stillness, spirits weave,
Ghostly threads we dare believe.
Shimmering whispers fill the air,
Tales of those no longer there.

Flickering candles, shadows play,
Ghostly figures dance away.
In their wake, a soft refrain,
Calling forth, with love, not pain.

Threads of silver, pathways bright,
Guide the lost through endless night.
Every flicker tells a story,
Of shadows wrapped in fleeting glory.

Echoes linger in the gloom,
As they weave through warmth and bloom.
Light will pierce the darkest dome,
In ghostly threads, we find our home.

With every shimmer, hope ignites,
In the depths of silent nights.
Threads of light and love unite,
Ghostly threads bring forth our sight.

A Tapestry of Ethereal Echoes

In the realm where shadows dwell,
Soft whispers weave the night's spell.
Stars twinkle in silent grace,
A dance of light in endless space.

Strings of fate in twilight spun,
Threads of dreams 'neath the dying sun.
Each echo tells a tale untold,
Of memories warm and secrets old.

Luminous threads through darkness creep,
Embracing hearts that yearn and weep.
A melody of the moonlit air,
Sweet serenades of love and care.

Reflections caught in gentle streams,
Swaying softly in the land of dreams.
A tapestry no eyes can see,
Yet felt in souls that long to be.

In every fiber, a heartbeat flows,
A luminous tale where time bestows.
A dance of echoes, forever bright,
In the mystical veil of the night.

Faint Flames of Dusk's Embrace

As daylight fades and shadows rise,
Faint flames flicker in the skies.
Whispers of dusk in crimson hue,
Promising dreams to be born anew.

Beneath the arch of twilight's hand,
Fireflies gather, softly planned.
Their glow, a language of the night,
In a world painted with fading light.

Branches sway, a hush descends,
Nature's song, a tune that blends.
The horizon, cloaked in deep indigo,
Holds the secrets dusk may bestow.

Candles flicker in distant homes,
As night-time beckons, softly roams.
Embers dance, a warm embrace,
In every corner, a sacred space.

Faint flames whisper promises near,
Of stories long and shadows dear.
In dusk's embrace, we find our place,
Bathed in warmth, lost in grace.

Glowing Veils in the Misty Reverie

Mist drapes softly over hills,
A shimmering breath, a silent thrill.
Veils of fog in moonlight's gleam,
Drawing forth the fragile dream.

Every step upon the moss,
Leaves behind a delicate gloss.
Whispers echo through the trees,
Carried softly by the breeze.

In this realm where shadows play,
Time slips past like grains of gray.
Images swirl, both near and far,
Guided gently by a distant star.

A reverie of glowing light,
Illuminates the heart of night.
In the mist, a magic dense,
Silent secrets cohere, immense.

With every breath, the world unfolds,
In gentle hues of silken golds.
Wrapped in veils of softest white,
We drift away, embraced by night.

The Haunting Gleam of Dimming Light

As day concedes to twilight's grasp,
The last rays linger, a fleeting clasp.
A haunting gleam on the horizon,
A farewell kiss, soft as a sighin'.

Echoing whispers of the sun's descent,
In every shadow, memories spent.
Colors fade, yet hearts ignite,
The beauty found in dimming light.

Silhouettes dance against the sky,
A tapestry of dreams gone by.
In the glow of the fading day,
Hope remains, though skies turn gray.

Each flicker holds a tale of yore,
Of laughter shared and love before.
In twilight's embrace, we reminisce,
Through haunting gleams, we find our bliss.

Night draws close, its chill outlined,
Yet warmth whispers, heart entwined.
In the dusk, a silent plea,
To treasure moments, wild and free.

Light Beneath the Ethereal Veil

In shadows cast by soft moonlight,
A dance unfolds, a dream takes flight.
Whispers carry through the trees,
Awakening the night's gentle breeze.

Glowing stars, they chase the dark,
Leaving trails of radiant spark.
Each flicker tells a tale untold,
Of magic woven, brave and bold.

Beneath the veil, the world holds still,
A secret longing, a silent thrill.
In twilight's hush, the heart can roam,
Finding solace, calling it home.

Mysteries wrap like a tender shroud,
In ethereal light, softly proud.
A web of dreams begins to weave,
In every breath, the night believes.

So linger here, let time suspend,
In this realm where shadows blend.
For in the light that hides so well,
Lies the promise of the eternal spell.

Murmurs of a Half-Light Reverie

In the glade where echoes play,
Half-light dances, guiding the way.
A soft sigh stirs the ancient trees,
Whispers carried on the breeze.

Fragments of dreams in faded hue,
Reflect the magic, soft and true.
Clarity found in the fog's embrace,
Revealing a hidden, sacred place.

Footsteps quiet on mossy ground,
In stillness, answers can be found.
The half-light holds a tender grace,
Inviting hope to find its space.

Veils of twilight gently unfold,
Entwining secrets, softly told.
In the silence of the night,
Dreamers gather, hearts alight.

Murmurs float like whispered song,
Binding souls where they belong.
In the half-light, we find our way,
To realms of peace where shadows play.

Lurking Beneath the Drifting Veil

Mists curl low in the quiet night,
Secrets linger, hidden from sight.
Lurking shadows drift and sway,
As the veils of silence softly play.

A haunting call from the distant sea,
Echoes of moments that used to be.
In the depths where feelings loom,
Hope flickers through the thickening gloom.

Beneath the veil, a truth concealed,
Waiting for hearts that long to be healed.
Softly whispering tales of old,
Of love's embrace and warmth untold.

Time dances in this ethereal space,
Memories glide, a haunting grace.
Through the mist, we weave our dreams,
Unraveling threads of moonlit seams.

Lurking softly in the pale glow,
Darkness dances, inviting the flow.
In this twilight, we find our peace,
A timeless bond, a sweet release.

The Enigma of Faint Radiance

A flicker caught in the evening air,
Whispers linger, sweet and rare.
Faint radiance spills through the trees,
Cradled in twilight's gentle breeze.

Echoes of laughter, slight and warm,
Surrounded by the sky's soft charm.
In the hush where shadows blend,
Light reveals what dreams intend.

The enigma glows, a puzzle to solve,
Guiding the heart as mysteries evolve.
Each gleam, a promise, tenderly sewn,
Binding the paths of the lost and known.

In this dance of dusk and dawn,
Faint radiance beckons, urging us on.
Through twisting paths, we carve our tale,
In light's embrace, we will not pale.

So chase the spark that calls to thee,
In the glow, we dare to be free.
The enigma whispers, softly bright,
Revealing truths in the tender night.

Whispering Lights of Dusk

The sun bows down, a gentle fade,
Soft whispers carry through the glade.
Colors blend in twilight's embrace,
Each moment holds a sacred space.

Fireflies flicker, a dance so bright,
Reminders of day's retreating light.
Breeze whispers secrets, trees softly sway,
Night's cloak drapes on the ending day.

Stars emerge, a blanket of dreams,
Mirroring the quiet moon's beams.
In this stillness, magic ignites,
Hope twinkles softly, a promise of nights.

Between the dusk and dreams that flow,
A canvas painted with soft glow.
Each light a story, a voice that sings,
Whispering hope as the night begins.

Embracing shadows, the world unwinds,
In the hush, the heart truly finds.
Connections made as the day departs,
Whispering lights weave through our hearts.

Luminescence Between the Shadows

In twilight's hush, a shimmer glows,
Between the shadows, light bestows.
A dance of dusk, so soft and light,
Every corner holds a glimpse of night.

Glimmers flicker from the leaves,
With each flick, the heart believes.
In silence deep, a story spins,
In every breath, the world begins.

Night blooms forth with gentle grace,
Filling spaces, a warm embrace.
Even shadows, with a flicker bright,
Hold the promise of sacred light.

Emerald hues and sapphire dreams,
In darkness flow, the starlight streams.
Dancing colors paint the air,
In luminescence, hearts lay bare.

Beyond the shadows, hope takes flight,
Illuminated by love's pure light.
Each echo whispers, soft yet bold,
In the realm where night unfolds.

Cloaked Threads of Luminescent Hues

Threads of dusk in deep shades spin,
Weaving tales where dreams begin.
Colors blend in silent halls,
A tapestry that softly calls.

Golden glows and whispers keen,
Blend with shadows, unseen, serene.
Soft blush paints the evening's face,
Crafting magic, time and space.

Cloaked in warmth, the night unfolds,
Secrets shared, and stories told.
With every hue, the heart replies,
In the dusk, the spirit flies.

Under starlight's gentle gleam,
Awakening each tender dream.
Luminescent notes drift and flow,
In the silence, peace will grow.

A dance of colors in the night,
Threads of beauty, soft and bright.
In each moment, we find our muse,
Cloaked in threads of luminescent hues.

Enchanted by the Glow of Dusk

As dusk descends, enchantment reigns,
A golden glow on amber plains.
Rustling leaves, a soothing song,
In this moment, we all belong.

Lights emerge like fire's embrace,
Casting shadows that softly trace.
With every flicker and fading light,
Mystery dances into the night.

The air is rich with fragrant dreams,
A world aglow, or so it seems.
In the twilight, hearts intertwine,
Touched by magic, the stars align.

Gentle murmurs of the deep,
As twilight whispers secrets to keep.
In the stillness, we find the spark,
Enchanted by dusk, lost in the dark.

Beyond the horizon, stars arise,
Painting hopes in the open skies.
In this glow, forever stays,
A memory woven in dusky rays.

Shrouded in a Luminous Veil

In the night's embrace, whispers unwind,
Stars flicker softly, secrets to find.
Moonlight dances on shadows that creep,
Wrapped in the silence, the world falls asleep.

Veils of mist swirl, cloaking the land,
Dreams drift and twirl like grains of sand.
A gentle breeze carries stories untold,
Of lovers and legends, of hearts made of gold.

Each petal ignites in a soft silver hue,
While echoes of past wrapped in silence renew.
Time weaves the threads of both dark and light,
As whispers of dawn chase away the night.

Ethereal visions on the horizon break,
Painting the heavens in hues soft and wake.
In this sacred moment, life breathes anew,
Shrouded in wonder, wrapped in the blue.

Elusive Echoes at Dusk

Just before twilight, silence unfolds,
Echoes of footsteps in stories retold.
As shadows stretch long and colors entwine,
The day gently whispers, its secrets divine.

Golden horizons blush, kissed by the night,
Crickets begin their soft concert of light.
A tapestry woven with threads made of dreams,
Hints at the magic in soft, murmured themes.

Stars blink awake, shy across the expanse,
Night wraps the earth in a velvet romance.
Elusive are moments, like whispers of air,
Drifting through stillness, with none left to share.

Time lingers gently, yet swift as a sigh,
In this sacred space, where moments lie.
Elusive echoes, a fading refrain,
Leave traces of wonder, a soft, sweet pain.

Secrets Carried by the Wisp

A flicker of light dances through the trees,
A wisp of a secret on the softest breeze.
It carries the tales of the ancients, the wise,
Where stories are hidden beneath starlit skies.

Glimmers of laughter, shadows of pain,
Memories huddled where no one can gain.
Drifting like smoke, these whispers reside,
In the heart of the night, where mysteries hide.

Secrets entwined in the thicket of dreams,
Flowing like water in silvery streams.
The world holds its breath as the wisp softly glows,
Unraveling stories the moonlight bestows.

Each flicker a promise, a piece of the past,
Carried through time, an echo steadfast.
Secrets unspoken, in shadows they stay,
With wisps guiding souls, lighting the way.

Where Twilight Meets the Ether

At the edge of the day, where twilight does blend,
Shadows and sunlight are destined to mend.
Colors collide in a mystical dance,
A moment of magic, a fleeting romance.

The horizon whispers with hues soft and bold,
Stories of old, eternally told.
A canvas of dreams paints the sky wide,
Where imagination and reality slide.

In this sacred space, hearts open wide,
Yearning for journeys where hopes can abide.
Time drifts like clouds on a gentle exhale,
As twilight embraces, a silken veil.

Stars peek from corners, shy and unsure,
Waiting to shimmer, waiting for more.
In the embrace of the night, we are free,
Where twilight meets ether, just you and me.

Phantoms of the Glistening Veil

In the twilight's soft embrace,
Whispers dance with moonlit grace.
Shadows play upon the ground,
Lost in dreams, they swirl around.

Misty figures weave and sway,
Glistening veil, where phantoms stay.
Echoes of a time long past,
Fleeting moments, shadows cast.

Each sigh carries tales untold,
Crafted in the silver mold.
They beckon forth with gentle hands,
Guiding through forgotten lands.

Brightly shining, yet concealed,
Magic's touch, a heart revealed.
Within the veil, a world unfolds,
A secret place where wonder holds.

In this twilight, spirits roam,
Phantoms searching for a home.
With each heartbeat, dreams awake,
In the veil, their paths will break.

Secrets in the Shimmering Fog

Beneath the cloak of misty air,
Secrets linger everywhere.
Veils of silence in the night,
Shimmering whispers take their flight.

Echoing through the vapor's dance,
Lost in thoughts, a fleeting glance.
Fog encircles, soft and deep,
Hiding truths that shadows keep.

Elusive forms that twist and turn,
In the stillness, long they yearn.
Unraveled tales of joy and woe,
Secret paths that few can know.

With each step, the mystery grows,
Hidden worlds, where nobody goes.
In this fog, time starts to bend,
Where past and future softly blend.

Secrets call from every side,
In the mist, where dreams abide.
Follow closely, heed the song,
For in the fog, you'll find where you belong.

Reflections on the Dusky Waters

In twilight's calm, the waters gleam,
Mirroring thoughts of a fading dream.
Softly whispered, the night descends,
Where time and shadow gently blend.

Ripples dance on a glassy lake,
Each reflection, a memory's wake.
Fading echoes of light and shade,
In dusky waters, secrets wade.

The horizon blushes with violet hues,
Painting stories the heart can choose.
Beneath the waves, whispers call,
Of distant lands and the rise and fall.

Stars emerge, a fragmented sight,
Twinkling softly in the night.
Their glow weaves through the liquid night,
Binding dreams in gentle light.

In these depths, the soul can find,
Celestial truths unconfined.
Reflections dance, forever sway,
In dusky waters, night meets day.

Embrace of the Silken Dusk

Wrapped in hues of muted gold,
The silken dusk begins to unfold.
A tender touch upon the skin,
As day departs, the night draws in.

Gentle sighs weave through the air,
Softly speaking of sweet despair.
Every shadow leans to share,
Intimate truths, a silent prayer.

In the fading light, hearts ignite,
Flickering hopes in dimming sight.
Wrapped in warmth, a fragile bliss,
The dusk invites a lover's kiss.

Whispers flutter like ancient leaves,
In the stillness, the silence weaves.
All the dreams too shy to speak,
Find their voice in twilight's peak.

So let the dusk enfold us tight,
In its embrace, we find our light.
Together we shall softly rest,
In the calm of the evening's best.

Glimmers in the Gloom

In shadows deep, the whispers flow,
Soft glimmers dance, where few may go.
A flicker bright, in darkened wet,
Hope's gentle spark, we won't forget.

Through tangled roots, the silence sighs,
As fading light bids night goodbye.
Each breath we take, as stars align,
In gloom we find, our hearts entwine.

The moon ascends, a silver thread,
We stride with dreams, where fears have fled.
With every step, the glow expands,
In hidden paths, we grasp our plans.

Beneath the weight of twilight's cloak,
A subtle truth in silence spoke.
The world unfurls, as night descends,
In shadows deep, our journey bends.

So stand with me, as night takes hold,
In every drop, the tales unfold.
We'll weave our hopes, in midnight's loom,
And find our way through glimmers' gloom.

Reflections on a Shrouded Path

On misty trails, the echoes hum,
Footsteps lost, where shadows come.
Reflections dance, in fleeting gleam,
Through shrouded paths, we chase a dream.

The trees whisper secrets, soft and low,
Guiding us gently, where few would go.
With every turn, the night enfolds,
In whispered tales, our spirit molds.

Veils of fog hug the winding way,
Each twist and turn, inviting play.
The heart beats loud, beneath the shroud,
As we wander, lost in the crowd.

A lantern's flicker, a moment's spark,
Illuminates the depths of dark.
In every shadow, a truth concealed,
On shrouded paths, our fate revealed.

So take my hand, together we'll roam,
In reflections found, we make a home.
Through veils of mist, our souls unite,
On this shrouded path, we chase the light.

Silhouetted Dreams in Twilight

In twilight's brink, our shadows play,
Silhouetted dreams, they drift away.
A canvas spun of dusky hues,
In fading light, our hearts infuse.

With every star that starts to bloom,
We paint the night, dispel the gloom.
A fleeting glance, a breathless sigh,
In twilight's veil, we learn to fly.

The world transforms as day meets night,
In whispered shades, we find our flight.
Amidst the calm, our hopes arise,
As visions dance in violet skies.

Each heartbeat swells, with life anew,
In silhouette, I stand with you.
Together bound, in dusk's embrace,
Our dreams take form, as shadows trace.

So climb with me, to heights unknown,
In twilight's grip, our spirits grown.
With silhouetted dreams in hand,
We leap and soar, just as we planned.

Embrace of the Fogbound Fable

Within the mist, a story stirs,
In fogbound fables, silence whirs.
Lines between truth, and dreams intertwine,
In whispered tales, our hearts define.

The fog envelops, a soft embrace,
Each step we take, a slow-paced race.
In hidden glens, where secrets thrive,
We share our hopes, and feel alive.

With every breeze, a voice we hear,
In gentle echoes, drawing near.
Legends woven in shadows' breath,
In fogbound worlds, we dance with death.

Through twilight's haze, our futures bind,
In every moment, the dreams we find.
While fog may cloak, it never steals,
The strength we cultivate, the truth it reveals.

So let us wander, side by side,
In fables rich, with hearts our guide.
Amidst the fog, our spirits gleam,
In this embrace, we seek our dream.

Enchanted by the Faint Luminosity

In twilight's soft, embracing glow,
Shadows dance where whispers flow.
Stars awaken, softly gleam,
Guiding hearts where dreamers dream.

A silver thread in night's embrace,
We wander through this timeless space.
With every step, the magic grows,
In gentle light, the spirit flows.

Secrets linger in the air,
Inviting souls to boldly dare.
The moonlit path begins to weave,
A tapestry where we believe.

Each flicker tells a tale untold,
Of whispered dreams and visions bold.
While night enfolds us in its arms,
We're captivated by its charms.

So let us dance till morning light,
Beneath the stars, our spirits bright.
Enchanted by this faint allure,
In luminous embrace, we are secure.

Veils of Glory Unseen

Behind the dark, a shimmer hides,
A world where endless beauty bides.
With every breath, the silence sings,
Of joy that only spirit brings.

Veils of glory hang like mist,
Each one cloaked in a lover's tryst.
Promises dance in muted light,
Calling forth the hidden sight.

In realms where shadows softly play,
We glimpse the dawn of a new day.
Threads of gold and silver bright,
Intertwine in the fading night.

The heart knows paths not walked before,
Through hidden doors, the spirits soar.
With every step, the world expands,
Veils lift softly at our hands.

So let us wander, hearts in flight,
Toward horizons kissed by light.
For in these veils, the truth is spun,
A dance of glory, never done.

Embracing the Lure of the Obscured

Beneath the shadows, mysteries dwell,
Where secrets linger, soft as a spell.
In the silence, whispers beckon near,
Inviting us to face our fear.

The beauty lies in what we can't see,
In every fold of unknown mystery.
Through tangled paths, where echoes abide,
We embrace the shadows, and let them guide.

With hearts wide open, we take the leap,
Into the depths, where silence keeps.
The lure of obscured pulls us in,
A journey through losses, a journey to win.

In twilight's hold, we find our grace,
In hidden corners, we find our place.
Every stumble shapes the soul's design,
Palettes of twilight, where stars align.

Let go the light that blinds us so,
Embrace the dark; it's where we grow.
With every shadow, a glimmer shines,
A path of wonder, where light entwines.

Ethereal Light Through Misty Veils

Through misty veils, a soft light glows,
Awakening dreams as the stillness grows.
Ethereal whispers in the air,
Guide the heart to places rare.

Footsteps echo on the dew-kissed ground,
In this haven, lost souls are found.
A flicker of hope in every breath,
Life's tender promise, even through death.

The dawn breaks slow, a gentle rise,
Painting the world with tender sighs.
In light's embrace, the shadows recede,
Every heart finds what it needs.

Misty veils unveil the day,
A soft reminder of love's array.
With every beam, the world ignites,
An endless dance of silent nights.

So we wander, hand in hand,
Through this dreamlike, enchanted land.
Ethereal light, forever near,
Guiding our spirits, calm and clear.

Gossamer Veils and Distant Stars

In twilight's glow, soft whispers weave,
Gossamer veils that night will grieve.
Stars above in silent tears,
Dance like dreams, void of fears.

The moon spills light on silver streams,
While shadows cradle gentle dreams.
Each flicker speaks of love lost,
A testament to the heart's cost.

The winds carry tales of the past,
Echoes of lovers that couldn't last.
They twine through branches, soft and frail,
In the embrace of night's sweet veil.

Yet hope persists in the cosmos high,
Forging paths where souls can fly.
Through gossamer strands that intertwine,
Hearts shall meet in realms divine.

The night unfolds with starlit grace,
Shimmering worlds in a fleeting space.
With every glance, with every prayer,
We find our way in the night air.

Light's Caress in the Misty Echo

Beneath the shroud of morning mist,
Light's caress, a tender twist.
Echoes linger, soft and clear,
Whispers of the dawn draw near.

The sun peeks through a curtain grey,
A golden touch to greet the day.
Droplets glisten on grass so bright,
Dancing jewels in warming light.

Memories float on the gentle breeze,
Carried softly through swaying trees.
Each breath taken, a sacred pause,
In nature's embrace, we find our cause.

Birds awaken with songs of cheer,
Filling the air, their message clear.
Life begins in every ray,
A promise kept, come what may.

So let the echoes guide your soul,
In every moment, feel the whole.
With light's caress, we are alive,
In misty realms, our spirits thrive.

Enchanted Murk and Velvet Nights

In enchanted murk, shadows play,
Whispers of dreams, where night holds sway.
Velvet drapes the world in dusk,
Breathing secrets, rich and musk.

Stars emerge as candles bright,
Illuminating the path of night.
Each twinkle tells a story old,
Of heartbeats shared, of love untold.

The world quiets with a velvet sigh,
As time drifts like smoke, floating by.
With every flicker, we draw near,
Finding solace in what we fear.

Embrace the dark, the hidden grace,
For within it lies a sacred place.
Where wishes thrive and shadows dance,
In enchanted dreams, we take a chance.

So let the murk wrap 'round your heart,
Where stillness weaves a magic art.
In velvet nights, we dare to dream,
Awakening hope's soft gleam.

Flickers within the Nebulous Realm

In the nebulous realm, shadows play,
Flickers of light in the cosmic sway.
Galaxies spin in a silent waltz,
Crafting tales with no faults.

Stars like gems on a canvas vast,
Whispering secrets of the past.
Through the dark, they weave a thread,
Connecting souls, both alive and dead.

The universe breathes, a fragile sigh,
Embracing wonders that soar high.
Each flicker, a spark of fate,
Guiding the lost, never too late.

In the depths of night, we find our way,
Through nebulae that gently sway.
Existence pulses, a mystic dream,
Binding us all in the cosmic stream.

So let us dance in this sacred space,
With every flicker, feel love's grace.
Within the realm, together we soar,
In the heart of the stars, forevermore.

www.ingramcontent.com/pod-product-compliance
Lightning Source LLC
Chambersburg PA
CBHW070025020125
19746CB00003B/84

9 789908 163970